THE FOUR KEYS
TO IMPROVE YOUR GAME

THE PRO'S WAY TO
PLAY BETTER GOLF

TIM CUSICK

Published by Charles Pinot
Designed by Angela Conant

First Printing, 2014
10 9 8 7 6 5 4 3 2 1

DEDICATION

I have been writing this book for twenty years. Not on paper but in my mind through training, work experiences, thousands of lessons, clinics, golf schools and speaking engagements. I never formalized my thoughts until a good friend of mine Deb Mielke encouraged me to do so late in the fall of 2012. As you'll see in the book she has been a student of mine for a number of years. Deb helped with the initial book concept, editing and picture design of the book.

Most of my formal training in golf came under the tutelage of Hank Haney. I had the good fortune to teach with and for him for 23 years. Hank shaped my skills, style and work ethic for making golfers better at playing the game of golf. His wisdom will always be with me for as long as I teach this great game.

Since 2002 I've written a golf instruction article for a Dallas based golf magazine Avid Golfer. The Publisher of the magazine, Craig Rosengarden, has given me a platform to share my teaching ideas with his readers. This monthly formal writing exercise allowed me to hone my literally skills and to put my golf instruction thoughts on paper. Craig's photographer, Jason Wesch, always makes me look good in the monthly photos for Avid Golfer. In doing all the photography for the book, Jason outdid himself with his artistic skills of presenting golf instruction.

My current employer, the Four Seasons Resort and Club at Las Colinas was very gracious to allow me to shoot all the photos for the book on their property. They gave me a wonderful opportunity to become their Director of Golf Instruction in 2005.

Another student and friend of mine, Cash Nickerson, put me in touch with Charles Pinot Publishing. Cash was instrumental in helping me obtain the book agreement with "CP." Additionally I've been associated with Cash through his foundation, David H. Nickerson Foundation, www.davidscure. com. David's Cure works to raise awareness and to help find a cure for Prostate Cancer. A disease that my father, Mike, contracted a number of years ago and am happy to say is in remission. A portion of my profit from each book is going to go to David's Cure.

Finally, this book is dedicated to my wife Vicki and our son Carson. Writing this book would not have happened without the love and understanding I receive each and every day from them. They, unselfishly, have allowed me to pursue my career of teaching golf and sharing my expertise with my students during all hours of the day.

CONTENTS

FOREWORD

I worked down range from Tim for many years when he taught at The Hank Haney Golf Ranch and I was the club-fitter. That makes this forward personal as opposed to two guys in the same industry. Furthermore Tim is originally from Rochester NY and being originally from Syracuse myself we Yankees stuck together. I mean this in a good way, the Haney Ranch was very intense, or maybe better said golf intense. Everything got maximum effort be it details in instruction or attention to the equipment used.

As I watched Tim work as an instructor I became very impressed with the results he was getting. I used to threaten to take lessons from him myself but at his urging kept quiet lest I ruin his growing reputation.

A club called The Tight Lies was developed there and as it gained in popularity I handed off my club-fitting duties and became totally involved in Adams Golf. For all practical purposes this decision lasted for a 10 year period where I essentially gave up playing.

Then it was like, "Ok I think I'll play" except for one thing, unless you are sublimely talented you do not walk away for 10 years and return with any degree of success and sublimely talented I am not. Further, I had never taken lessons, more the occasional tip and to start playing again I needed a serious effort.

My first thought was Tim and by then he had moved to The Four Seasons Resort and Club/Dallas. I contacted him and told him that his reputation was well enough established that it was time to take on a major challenge, me.

I was a specific challenge, a decent player at one time, now older

(60) physically less flexible and needing a solid foundation to build upon. As you'll see by reading this book he delivers, not gimmicky fixes but cornerstones. I've said many times over the years that one of the great benefits being associated with the golf business is you get to meet some truly good people. Tim Cusick is one and moreover, he knows his stuff.

Barney Adams
Founder of Adams Golf

Chapter 1

WHERE GOLFERS GET LOST

It all started with the color commentator Dick Vitale. Before every televised college basketball game, Vitale introduced his "four keys" to winning for each team. Vitale's "keys" were simple, yet provided fans with great insights into the teams, their respective strengths and weaknesses.

Watching a game some years ago, I wondered, "Why isn't analyzing a golf swing as simple as analyzing a basketball game? Why aren't there four keys to analyzing the golf swing?"

As I worked with my students over the next few weeks, Dick's "four keys" were running through my mind. But the keys did not come into focus for me until a new student with a particularly unusual swing arrived for a lesson. As he warmed up, I concentrated more closely than ever on ball flight and impact. I was a surprised to find that with increased attention to these two areas, I was better able to spot the flaws in the student's swing. He had some big problems but once I had determined what his flaws were, fixing them was easy.

I came to realize that the best swing analysis doesn't come from the swing itself, it comes from analyzing four results of the swing.

- The trajectory of the ball in flight

- The curvature of the ball in flight

- Where the club face strikes the ball

- Impact

Once I had my "four keys" to analyzing the swing, the next step was to write down the flaws in a golfer's swing that cause, for example, a shank or a "sky ball". Now I had an easy-to-use chart that allowed me, simply by watching a few shots, to:

- Note trajectory, curvature, club face contact and impact

- Spot flaws associated with classic problems like a low hook

- See the best approach to correcting the mistake

By watching key aspects of a golfer's swing — trajectory, curvature, club face contact, impact — I could have an immediate and positive impact on a player's game. Using my "four keys," my students began to progress at an even faster pace.

It was then that I understood that nearly every golfer has the same problems. They know they have a swing flaw because they can see they're not hitting good shots. They look for answers, but answers aren't always easy to find. They get a tip from one of the golf magazines, and it might even work for a while, but at the end of a round they still aren't hitting the kind of shots they're capable of. They're lost. However, when golfers understand the "four keys" – trajectory, curvature, club face contact, impact – and the technical flaws that affect these key areas, they improve their swing and enjoy the game of golf a lot more.

So thanks Dick Vitale! Your pre-game tips for sports fans made a better golf instructor out of me. Your "four keys" inspired me to write a book that can help golfers of all ages and abilities improve their games.

Chapter 2

UNDERSTANDING THE FOUR KEYS

TRAJECTORY

A few years ago during the HP Byron Nelson Championship, I stood on the driving range with one of my students. As we watched the tour players warm up, my student commented on the speed, rhythm, and grace of their swings. He loved the results too, every shot was straight and every iron sounded crisp.

"How can you possibly teach these guys?" he asked. "They swing so fast it's hard to see anything."

"I don't watch the swing." I replied. "I watch the result. The characteristics of the shot help me diagnose where the problem is. Is the ball going too high? Is it curving too much? That's what I'm looking for. Once I see the result, I can zero in on the problem."

THE FOUR KEYS

Every golf shot has four basic characteristics. They're the "keys" to diagnosing and correcting swing flaws. They are:

- *Trajectory* – the height of the shot in relation to the club used

- *Curvature* – the shape of the shot (right or left) in flight

- *Club face contact* – the place on the club face that strikes the ball

- *Impact* – where the ball is struck in relation to the ground

The unique traits of every golfer's swing generate the trajectory, curvature, club face contact and impact of every shot. When something goes wrong, the result might be a "sky ball" off the tee, a hook or slice, a shank, or a "chunk." By understanding swing flaws that result in shots that don't have the correct trajectory, curvature, club face contact, and impact, golfers can study their shot, determine a possible cause for problems they are experiencing, and then, with the drills I've included in Chapter 6, correct nearly any problem.

TRAJECTORY

Trajectory is simply the loft or height of the shot. Every club has its own trajectory that is based on:

- Loft of the club

- Swing speed

- Angle of attack at impact

- What the clubface is doing at impact

The optimal trajectory is when the ball climbs and carries at the same time. Hit the ball too high and it won't carry. Hit the ball too low and it will fall out of the air and hit the ground too soon. In either case, the result is a loss of distance. The photo below illustrates different trajectories. The correct trajectory climbs and carries – and goes the furthest.

Specific swing traits either add to or subtract from the height of the shot. These traits can include:

Figure 1
Trajectory

Figure 2
Ball Position at Address

THE FOUR KEYS TO IMPROVING YOUR GAME

- *Ball position at address* – For right-handed golfers, the ball should be positioned in line with the player's nose for irons, and the left eye for hybrids, fairway woods and the driver. The butt end of the club should point to a spot just left of your navel and the shaft should fall in a straight line that is parallel to the ball. If the ball is positioned too far forward in the stance, the club will rise as it nears impact. This creates a higher, more lofted shot. Although this is the right ball position for hitting a shot that must carry over a big tree, it isn't the best position for a shot that you want to have climb *and* carry.

  When the ball is positioned too far back in the stance, the club will still be descending as it nears impact. The result is a lower, less lofted shot. Shots with less loft are great for chipping, playing wind shots and punching out of the trees—but, they aren't going to go as far as a normal shot.

- *Club head speed* – Generating club head speed is essential to getting the ball up in the air. It's a lot like an airplane at takeoff. If the plane doesn't have enough speed, it can't take off. If a golfer can't generate enough club head speed, the ball won't go very high. And if it can't go very high, it won't go very far.

Figure 3
Incorrect and Correct Swing Length

- *Swing length* – Trajectory is also determined by swing length. Shorter swings result in lower shots, longer swings in higher shots.

A good, full-swing shot trajectory is produced when the club is swung over the right shoulder in the backswing and over the left shoulder on the follow through. If the swing is abbreviated on either side of the ball, the shot will lose trajectory—and distance.

Figure 4
Club Face Loft
LEFT *clubface closed,* **CENTER** *clumbface open,* **RIGHT** *clubface square*

- *Club face loft* – Every clubface has a loft that is designed to produce a specific trajectory and distance based on club head speed and angle of attack at impact. To optimize each club's loft and trajectory, the club face must maintain the same loft at impact that it had at address.

  When the club face is de-lofted during the swing or at impact, the result is a shot that is too low. De-lofting is usually caused by a grip that is too strong or becomes too strong during the swing, a lack of club face rotation in the backswing, or a club face that closes before impact.

  When too much loft is added to the club face at impact, shots go too high. This problem is usually caused by a grip that is too weak or weakens during the swing, a backswing with excessive club face rotation, or a club face that is too open or opening at impact.

- *Loft created by the body* – To create good shot trajectory, the

Figure 5
Unbalanced Swings

body must be in the proper position throughout the swing.

○ At address, with irons the head should be centered over the ball; slightly behind the ball with fairway metals and the driver.

○ During the backswing, your weight shifts onto the right side as the head moves to a spot slightly behind the ball.

○ At impact, with irons your weight shifts back to the left side as the head returns to a spot even with the ball; slightly behind the ball with fairway metals and the driver.

○ At the finish, your weight shifts almost completely to the left side as your head rotates to look for the ball. Improper body movement can create a low trajectory when there is too much weight on the left side at address or at

Figure 6
Weight on Left Side - Low Trajectory Shot

Figure 7
Weight on Right Side - High Trajectory Shot

the top of the backswing. Additionally, if the head or upper body turns through too quickly on the downswing, a lower shot can result.

Conversely, when the head is tilted too far back or there is too much weight on the right side at address, a higher shot is produced. More loft is also created when the body stays behind the ball at impact and at the finish.

Figure 8
Correct and Incorrect Swing Angles
LEFT *from the outside,* **CENTER** *correct swing angle,*
RIGHT *too much from the inside*

- *Loft created by the swing angle* – Shot trajectory is also created by direction or the angle of the club as it swings back and through. Because golfers stand to the side of the ball, the club must swing on an arc that goes inside and up over the right shoulder on the backswing, down from the inside to square up at impact, and then up the inside on the follow through. Swing analyses that were performed using TrackMan launch monitors found shot trajectories are optimized when the swing varies no more than two degrees from the inside and one degree from outside the target line on the downswing.[1]

When the downswing is too steep and to the left of the target, the ball is trapped and the shot loses loft (and distance). When, however, a swing is angled too much up and to the right, a high shot with little carry is produced.

Chapter 3

UNDERSTANDING THE FOUR KEYS

CURVATURE

Curvature is the ball's movement to the right or left of the target while in flight. The initial direction of the shot is controlled by where the club face contacts the ball. (For example, if the downswing comes from inside the target line, the clubface closes and contacts the outside of the ball, and the ball will start to the left of the intended target line even though the club path was angled to the right. Conversely, if the downswing comes from inside the target line and contacts the inside of the ball with the face open, the ball will start to the right of the target line.) Once direction is established, curvature is magnified by:

- The loft of the club face

- The angle of the swing path at impact

- The angle of the club face at impact

How much the shot curves is determined by the difference between the angle of the swing path and the angle of the club face at impact. Shots with big curves to the right (slices) or the left (hooks) have big variations between the angles of the swing path and the club face at impact. (For example, a "boomerang hook" off the tee occurs because the loft of the club is low, the angle of the swing is out and to the right, and the club face is massively closed to the direction of swing path. There is a very large difference between the angles of the swing path [right] and the club face [closed or left].)

- **Ball Curving Too Much to the Right (the Slice)**

  The biggest problem for most golfers is a shot that curves to the right resulting in a **slice**. Slices often result in shots that sail into the trees or out of bounds and don't go very far. They're caused by a club face that is open or in the process of opening at impact.

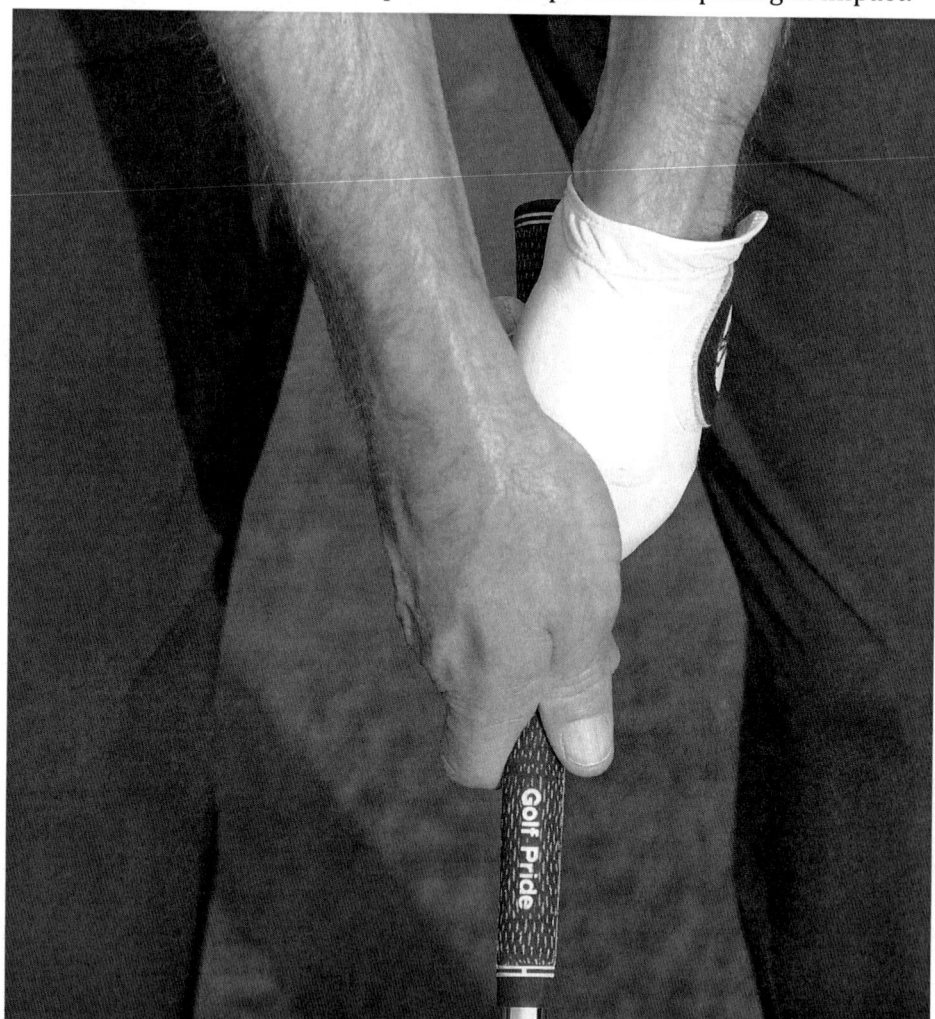

Figure 9
Weak Grip

This is usually triggered by:

- *A weak grip:* Players with good grips should see no more than two knuckles on their left hand at address (if you are a right-handed player). The right palm should cover up the left thumb and the "V's" that are formed by the thumb and first finger should point toward the right shoulder. With a

Figure 10
Body Ahead of Arms and Hands

Figure 11
Upright Swing

weak grip, however, the hands are turned too much to the left (for a right-handed player). Weak grips open the club face and keep it open throughout the swing.

- o *A tight grip:* Clutching the club in a stranglehold creates tight arms. Tight arms restrict the golfer's ability to release and square the club at impact. The result is usually an open club face upon impact.

- o *Body motion:* On the downswing, the upper body should stay turned as the downswing begins to allow the hands, arms, and the club to play "catch up" at impact. However, when the upper body starts the downswing or gets too far ahead of the arms and hands during the downswing, the club face tends to open at impact and create a slice.

- o *Upright swing:* When the swing is too upright, the arms have a tendency to counter-rotate as they approach impact. This action opens the club face and creates a big curve to the right.

- • **Ball Curving Too Much to the Left (the Hook)**
  The hook is the exact opposite of the slice. At impact the club face is closed or closing. Hitting the ball too far to the left is usually a problem for better players whose backswings are "on plane" and who understand how to use their arms, hands, and body to release the club. Hooks happen because:

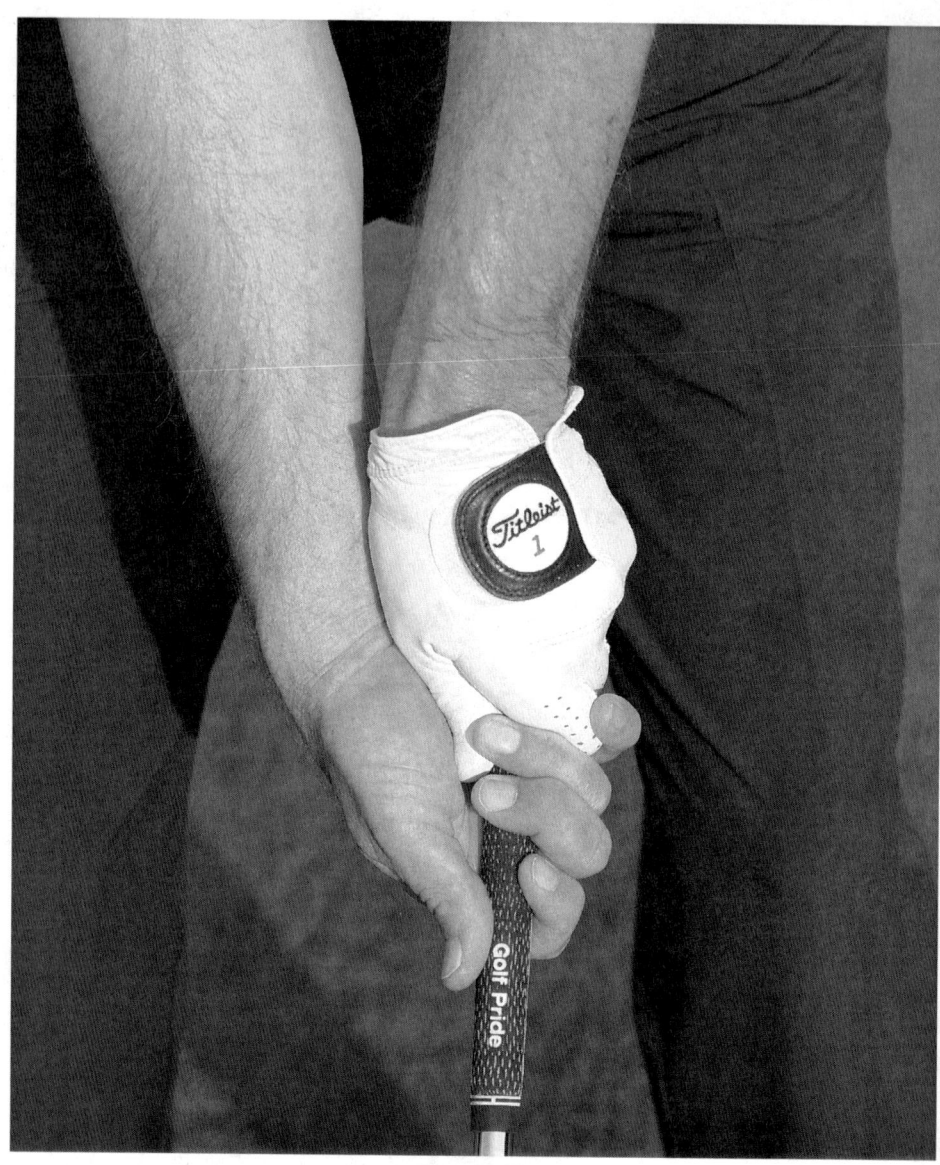

Figure 12
Strong Grip

- *The grip is too strong:* With a strong grip, the hands are turned too much to the right (for right-handed players). This usually keeps the club faced closed throughout the swing.

Figure 13
Hands Too Active

o *The hands are too active:* When the hands and club move
   faster than the body, the club face is usually closed at
   impact. Players need to speed up their legs, hips, and torso
   to enable the club face to stay open a little longer which will
   reduce or eliminate their hooks.

Figure 14

LEFT too much from inside, RIGHT correct angle

○ *The swing is coming into the ball too much from the inside:*
This problem can be a bit confusing. The path of the club is
underneath the plane and to the right. However, since the
club face strikes the outside of the ball, the shot hooks to
the left. Where the club face strikes the ball can override
the path of the swing.

Chapter 4

UNDERSTANDING THE FOUR KEYS
CLUB FACE CONTACT

There's nothing like the sound and feel of a shot that hits the center of the club face. It's what golfers live for. However, when the ball strikes the perimeter of the club face, the vibration can cause the club face to open or close. Contact that is too high or low on the face produces shots with poor trajectory. And *any* shot that doesn't hit the center will lose distance. Therefore, it's important to understand what causes golfers to miss the center and hit on the toe, heel, bottom, or top of the club face.

- *Toe and heel hits:* It's never fun to hit the ball off the toe or heel of the club face. The ball doesn't carry very far and, on a cold

Figure 15
Heel and Toe Hits

day, the vibration from a toe or heel hit can send a shock wave right up your arms.

Heel hits however, are a bigger problem than those hit off the toe. Why? Because heel hits are dangerously close to the hosel of the club. Anyone who's ever hit a "shank" knows how important it is to move contact back to the center of the club face.

There are five very different reasons as to why golfers hit the ball off of the toe or heel of the club face. The first reason doesn't have anything to do with the swing.

- *Clubs that don't fit:* Golf clubs are built to fit the "average" U.S. male or female. On average, that means a man who is 5'10" or a woman who is 5'4". Assuming a male player is 5'10" and doesn't have unusually long or short arms, standard clubs will be a great fit. However, if the player is 5'11" or taller, he may need clubs that are longer and/or have a more upright lie.

  Players using clubs that are too short or have too flat of a lie will usually hit the ball off the toe of the club face. Clubs that are too long or upright will usually force a player to hit the ball off the heel. I advise my students to adjust the lie of their clubs no more than two degrees upright or two degrees flat of standard lie. Unless you are taller than 6'4" or shorter than 5'0", this adjustment range is a good guideline. And I always advise my students to visit a certified club fitter or PGA Golf Professional *before* they purchase new equipment.

Figure 16
Club Lengths and Lie

o *Stance at address:* It's hard to hit the center of the club face from a stance that is too far away or too close to the ball. Players who have too much weight on their heels or don't bend enough at the knees and hips at address tend to hit the ball off the toe of the club.

Players that lean too far over their toes or bend too much at the hip are too close to the ball. They are therefore prone to hit the ball off the heel of the club.

Figure 17
Address Position - Toe and Heel Hits

o In a good setup, the weight is on the balls of the player's feet, the knees are slightly flexed, and the torso is bent at the hips. The tops of the player's shoulders should be in line with the front of their kneecaps.

o *Incorrect body motion:* Toe and heel hits are often the result of motions that move the body or club away from or toward the ball. Body motions that promote toe hits include:

- *Weight shifts toward the heels*

- *Shoulders opening too soon at the start of the downswing*

- *"Looking up" before impact*

- *Any body part that straightens*

- *Arms and hands pull in toward the body*

- *Body motions that produce heel hits include:*

- *Body moving closer to the ball*

- *Falling into the ball with the head*

- *Moving into the ball with the knees*

Figure 18
Body Motions that Cause Toe and Heel Hits

o *Swinging in (toe hits) or out (heel hits) with the arms:* Many slicers attempt to correct their slice by using the direction of their swing—from way inside the target line. They don't correct the problem that causes the slice they just hit the ball off of the toe instead!

Outward movement by the arms—and subsequent heel hits—are usually the result of a backswing that is too flat or comes too much from the inside on the downswing. It can also originate from the right side as it turns into the shot at the start of the downswing.

Figure 19
Arm Swing Direction - Heel and Toe Hits

○ *Club "stuck behind" in the downswing:* This is a problem usually reserved for low-handicap golfers. When the club swings down too much from the inside, the toe will catch the outside of the ball when the club head releases.

• *Hits low or high on the club face:* There's an old saying, "thin to win." That's because shots hit low on the club face are very close to being really good ones. They just fly a bit lower than one hit in the center of the club face.

However, there aren't many good results from shots that are hit high on the club face. The usual result is the dreaded "chunk." As with toe and heel hits, the reasons for contact being high or low on the club face vary considerably. The five primary reasons are:

Figure 20
Club Stuck Behind

- *Clubs that don't fit:* Clubs that are too short make it difficult to get down to the ball. If they're too long, the divots might look like ditches.

- *Stance at address:* Stances that don't have enough bend at the hips and knees or where the weight is primarily on the heels, rarely take a divot.
  Upright swings usually produce hits that are very high on the face. Another reason for a "chunk" is a ball that is above the feet at address (it's closer!). Using a shorter club or choking down and standing slightly taller at the knees and hips helps to offset the lie.

- *Ball position too far forward or back at address:* From the forward position, the ball is struck by the club as it starts to rise. The result is a thin or topped shot.
  When it's too far back the ball is contacted when the club is still descending, causing a hit higher up on the clubface.

- *Swing that is too flat or upright:* Swings that are flat don't have enough "up," and won't have enough "down" to get to the ball. Contact will be low on the club face.
  Upright backswings result in straight-down downswings with contact high on the club face.

- *Incorrect body motion:* Moving up with any part of the body makes it hard to get back down to the ball. Dropping down or moving any body part toward the ball usually results in a hit that is high on the club face.

Chapter 5

UNDERSTANDING THE FOUR KEYS

IMPACT

Tour players have almost perfect impact. They make contact with the ball and the ground at the same time. Their divots are shallow, the same depth from start to finish, and square to the target. Because tour players make consistently good impact, they can make extraordinary shots. A good example is one of my students from the 1990s, Bruce Crampton. Bruce was a winner of fourteen events on the PGA Tour and twenty more on the Champions Tour.

One summer, we played a round together at PGA West's Stadium Course. On the third hole, Bruce hooked his tee shot into the fairway bunker on the left side of the fairway. With 235 yards to the green, and a fairly high lip to navigate, Bruce took out his three-wood. I couldn't wait to see the result—after all, a three-wood out of the bunker!

Bruce hit a perfect draw onto the green that ended up twenty feet from the hole.

I asked him, "What did you do differently for that shot?"

Bruce looked at me with a blank stare and said "Why would I do anything different?"

Bruce knew that he'd make perfect impact—even with a three-wood out of a fairway bunker.

Impact is all about taking a divot of the correct depth (shallow) and getting to the bottom of the downswing at the right place (ball and ground

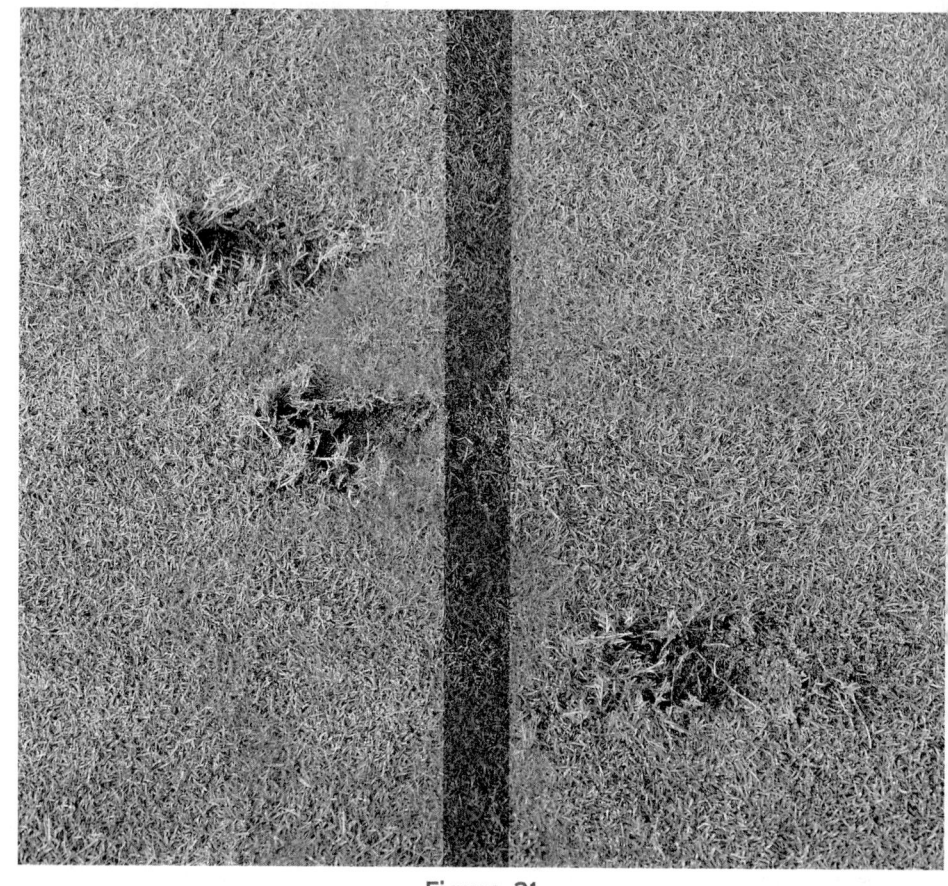

Figure 21
Divots

at the same time). When that doesn't happen:

- *Divots are too deep:* If the divot is deep, possible reasons include (since we've covered most of these symptoms in the other "keys," I'll be brief):

  o *A swing that is too steep*

  o *The body is moving down*

  o *The club is too long*

- *Divots are too shallow (or non-existent):* If the divot is shallow or non-existent it's likely that:

  o *The swing is too flat*

  o *Your body is lifting up*

  o *The club is too short*

- *Contact is behind the ball:* If the club strikes behind the ball:

  o *The swing is too flat*

  o *The hands and arms are moving faster than the body on the downswing*

  o *The hands have released too soon*

  o *The ball is positioned too far forward at address*

- *Contact is in front of the ball:* This is a better miss than is contact behind the ball. Contact is made in front of the ball when:

  o *The swing is too steep*

  o *Your body is turning too fast during the downswing*

  o *Your hands have released too late*

  o *The ball is too far back at address*

It should be clear by now that by observing the flight of the ball (trajectory and curvature), where the ball makes contact on the club face (toe/heel, low/high), and checking the divot for depth (deep, non-existent) and position (in front, behind), players can quickly diagnose the issues that are causing them to hit bad shots.

But before we get to the "fixes" in the next chapter, I've included a chart that summarizes the tips we've covered. This chart is a great tool to take to the range and it's the one I use whenever I have a new student.

TRAJECTORY

Too High

- Ball position at address is too far forward

- Fast swing speed

- Weak grip

- Adding loft with the body

- Angle of the swing up and to the right

- Big swing

Too Low

- Ball position at address is too far back

- Slow swing speed

- Strong grip

- Removing loft with body

- Angle of the swing is down and to the left

- Small swing

CURVATURE

To the Right

- Weak grip

- Tight grip

- Upper body starts downswing

- Upper body ahead of arms and hands on downswing

- Upright swing

To the Left

- Strong grip

- Loose grip

- Hands are too active

- Flat Swing. Swing coming into the ball too much from the inside

- Lower body slow to turn thru in downswing

CLUB FACE CONTACT

Toe Hit

- Clubs are too short or have too flat a lie

- Stance is too far away from the ball

- Weight shifts toward heels during the swing

- Shoulders open too soon at the start of the downswing

- "Looking up" before impact

- Straightening of any body part

- Arms and hands pull in toward body on downswing

- Club "stuck behind" in the downswing

Heel Hit

- Clubs that are too long or upright

- Stance is too close to the ball

- Falling into the ball with the head

- Moving into the ball with the knees

- Swinging out with the arms

High on Clubface Hit

- Clubs are too long

- Ball position too far back at address

- Upright swing

- Moving down or dropping any part of the body during the swing

Low on Clubface Hit

- Clubs are too short

- Not enough bend at the hips or knees at address

- Ball position too far forward at address

- Swing that is too flat

- Moving up any part of the body during the swing

IMPACT

Deep Divots

- Upright, steep swing

- Body is moving down during swing

- Clubs are too long

Shallow or No Divot

- Swing is too flat

- Body is lifting up during the swing

- Clubs are too short

Contact Behind the Ball

- Swing is too flat

- Hands and arms are moving faster than the body during the downswing

- Hands have released too soon

- The ball is positioned too far forward at address

Contact in Front of the Ball

- Swing is too steep

- Body is turning too fast during the downswing

- Hands have released too late

- The ball is positioned too far back at address

Chapter 6

PUTTING THE FOUR KEYS TO WORK TO IMPROVE YOUR GAME

There's an old adage that says, "What you learn first, you learn best." Golf swings are particularly good examples of this.

From the moment you begin to swing the club, you are establishing the movements and motion that will become "your" swing. With every swing you make, you ingrain the tempo, technique, and length of your swing. This can, of course, mean that you are establishing good habits—or imbedding bad ones.

That is why good instruction is such an important element for beginning golfers. With the proper grip, setup, and swing motion, a beginner has a much better chance of improving at a steady pace, but, more importantly, becoming a better, more consistent player.

That consistency isn't built on hitting great shot after great shot. It's made from hitting shots that are "good misses." Good misses are shots that are acceptable and playable. They may not be perfect, but they won't hurt you either.

Bad shots, on the other hand, are the result of major swing flaws. They're the slices, hooks, tops, shanks, fat, and thin shots that end up in the water, out of bounds, or half way to the green. These are the shots players should seek to fix, minimize, or eliminate.

The goal therefore, is simple. Keep the good misses, get rid of the bad shots.

In other words, ***prioritize*** your swing fixes to eliminate your worst shot—the bad shot. Go after shots that curve too much to the right or left fly too low, hit on the toe or hosel, take divots six inches behind the ball or four inches in front of it. You can't fix everything, so fix the shot that is hurting you the most. Now that you've decided on which bad shot you want to correct, you can use the chart from Chapter 5 to help you determine the cause. A cause that is, again, based on one of the four keys:

- Clubface contact

- Impact

- Trajectory

- Curvature

With the cause diagnosed, you can use the following drills to help you improve your swing and eliminate the fault that is causing you to hit your worst shot. Then, once that shot is "fixed," move on to your next "worst shot." For even the best players this is a never ending process. However, it is one that will help you to improve your score and make the game more enjoyable.

CLUBFACE CONTACT

- **The Two Tee Drill:** Place a tee just outside the toe and just outside the heel of the club head. The goal is to hit the ball, missing both tees. If you hit the tee by the heel, your shot is off the toe; if you strike the tee by the toe, the shot is off the heel. For beginning golfers, I

Figure 22
Two Tee Drill

substitute a third tee for the ball. Once they strike the middle tee consistently, I introduce the ball.

- **The One Tee Drill:** If you are hitting the ball on the toe, place a tee just outside the ball. Make sure the tee is actually leaning against the ball! The goal is to make contact with the ball and the tee simultaneously—making contact with the center of the clubface.

- **The Basket Drill:** This drill is for players with the "shanks." Place a ball basket (plastic!) just outside the ball—close enough so that it can only be avoided by making contact with the center or toe of the club. The goal again is to strike the ball and not the basket. If you don't have a basket, a water bottle or a head cover can also be used.

Figure 23
Basket Drill

- **Ball Below the Feet Drill:** This drill is for players who are making contact with the bottom of the club. Find a lie that positions the ball below your feet. It doesn't have to be a big difference, just make sure that ball is lower than your feet. This lie will encourage you to swing the club more up and down as well as letting you stay in your posture so that you can reach the ball.

- **Hover the Club Drill:** To eliminate shots hit high on the club face, choke down slightly on the club, then address the ball with the club off the ground and even with the ball. The goal is to swing through impact level of the ball without hitting the ground.

IMPACT

- **Identify Impact:** You can determine where the ball is striking the clubface by covering it with tape or chalk or coloring the face with a "dry erase" marker.

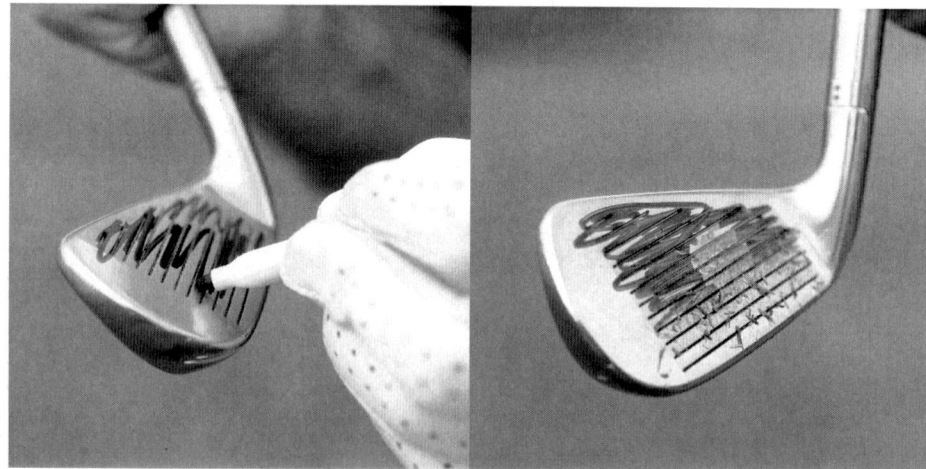

Figure 24
Identify Impact

- **Baseball Swing Drill:** This is a great drill for players who take deep divots or sky their tee shots. Starting at knee level, begin making swings above the ground, ensuring that the club swings back and through at your address position (knee level.) This drill develops a swing with more arc, minimizes divots, and improves clubface contact.

- **The Line Drill:** The goal of this drill is to improve the location of the bottom of the downswing. Draw a line where the ball would normally be, parallel to your clubface. Take a swing. Ideally, the bottom of the downswing should begin on the line, and the club should take a divot in front of the line. It's okay to start the divot slightly in front of the line, but never behind it.

- **Two-Club Drill:** This is another drill to improve the location of the bottom of the downswing. Hold a club in each hand, choking down to the end of the grip for better control. Very slowly, swing both clubs back and through, matching the shafts up with each other. This drill helps players improve their "feel" for the swing plane as the clubs move above, but remain parallel to, the plane established at setup. Swings that remain "on plane" generate solid impact with the ball and take a divot after contact.

Figure 25
Two-Club Drill

- **Towel Drill:** A great drill for

players who hit behind the ball. Place a towel one to two inches behind the ball. Attempt to make contact with the ball first, then the ground in front of the ball. This is a good drill to use after you've mastered the Line Drill outlined above.

- *Tee in Front of the Ball:* Another good drill for players who hit behind the ball. Push a tee three-quarters of the way into the ground and about one inch in front of the ball. Try to hit the ball so that you knock the tee out of the ground. This drill will help you move the bottom of your downswing forward.

TRAJECTORY

- *Uphill Slope Drill:* Players who hit the ball too low can use this drill to help them get the ball up in the air. Find a slight uphill slope, setting your body to match the slope. Place most of your weight on your right side (right-handed golfer). Let your downswing follow the path of the slope (do not swing into the slope!). The slope will help keep you from turning your upper body through too soon during the downswing. As a result, you'll get more height on all of your shots.

- *Smaller Swing Drill:* Players who hit the ball too high will like this drill. Swing the club only to shoulder height on both the backswing and the downswing. Shortening the swing helps lower a shot's trajectory. During the drill, change the length of your swing to discover how it affects the trajectory of the ball.

- *Variable Club Speed Drill:* This drill will help you to understand how the speed of your swing impacts ball trajectory. Begin by making a slow motion swing with a six- or seven-iron. Gradually increase the speed of your swing and note the difference in distance and trajectory until you reach half speed. Using this drill, you'll be able to control distance and trajectory with the speed of your swing.

- *Club Head Speed Drill:* Players who need to increase their club head speed can use this drill. Grip a club upside down and swing it through the air while maintaining good balance. The goal of the drill is to increase the sound the club makes as it swishes through the air. Once the sound has become louder, try to use that same speed when hitting the ball.

- *Ball Position Drill:* Optimal trajectory is also a result of good ball position at setup. To make sure you've got the ball in the right place, place one club down your foot line and another between your feet, even with your nose for irons, aligned with your left eye for woods. The two clubs will form a 'T.' Hit some shots!

- *Mirror Drill:* The position of the clubface throughout the swing has a significant impact on ball trajectory. To make sure that your clubface position is correct, practice swinging in a mirror. Start by making a grip without a club. Swing your arms and hands back to a point even with your chest. Open your hands as if you were going to clap. Envision a plane of glass between your hands matching the plane of your swing. Continue the "swing" to the top and then swing down to the same position, stopping at a place even with your chest. Your palms should open. Again, envision a plane of glass between your hands. This drill helps to provide the feeling of the proper arm and hand position throughout the backswing and downswing. Final note: make sure that your grip is neutral, not too strong or weak!

- **Weighted Club Drill:** Swinging a weighted club is an excellent way for a player with a short swing to get more height on their shots. Focus on letting the club swing up and over your right shoulder (if you are a right-handed player) and allow the wrists to cock the club down at the top of the backswing. Finish with the club up and over the left shoulder. The wrists should cock again to support the finish.

CURVATURE

- **Feet Together Drill:** This drill helps improve release of the club. It's especially effective for slicers! Position your feet next to each other, then swing the club back and through without a body turn. Taking your body out of the swing will help you release the club better!

- **Hips and Legs Drill:** Players who hit a lot of hooks will love this drill. Make sure your grip is neutral. Then swing, focusing on clearing the hips with the right thigh moving toward the left thigh (if you are a right-handed golfer), with the right heal releasing off the ground. At the finish, the belt buckle should face the target, the right thigh should squeeze gently against the left thigh, and the right foot should be straight up and down. This movement helps to hold the clubface open longer through impact, thereby reducing the chance of a hook.

- **Back to the Target Drill:** This is another good drill for slicers. Address the ball and turn your body to the right, but not so far you can't reach the ball. Swing the club up and over your right shoulder with your hands and arms. Then, let the club swing back down through impact. The follow through will be somewhat restricted. However, by keeping your back to the target, the club will swing down from inside the target line, and the hands and arms will release the club.

TENDENCIES

The Four Keys and the drills outlined previously will help players correct their mistakes and improve their games. However, the drills aren't a "cure all." In golf, every day is different. What worked yesterday may not work today. That terrible round you had last week doesn't mean you won't play well today. Because we're human, our feelings, capabilities and rhythm are always changing. That explains why a tour professional might shoot 74 on their first round, but then fire a 65 in the second.

Swings can vary for a number of reasons. Weather, personal matters, sleep, diet, and surroundings are all elements that can affect play or practice. That's why it's important to prepare for a round of golf or even a practice session. You'll find that with a plan in place for your round or practice session, you'll achieve more and will improve more quickly.

During your round or practice session, note your rhythm, balance, and the motion of your swing. Every round or session should also include an image, feeling or thought that will help you hit quality shots. Remember your tendencies and focus on the areas that will help you avoid bad shots.

As you warm up use your first fifteen to twenty balls to get a feel for what is happening. Are your rhythm and balance okay or do they need some attention? Maybe your swing doesn't feel just right. If so, it's time to work on the things that will improve your swing. And maybe, on one of your really good days, everything will feel great. That's when you want to stay *in the moment* as long as you can!

Don't let cell phones or other golfers distract you! Soak in every good shot by holding your finish just a moment longer. Watch every good shot and then try to replicate it. It's important to store the images of good shots in your mind so that you can recall them when you're on the course or in a tournament.

Unfortunately, rounds and practice sessions that start out great often deteriorate due to a lack of physical or mental energy. Therefore it's important to pace yourself, allowing for breaks to rest, drink plenty of water, and eat something healthy. This simple formula will ensure that you have the energy you'll need to keep performing at a high level throughout the round or practice.

Finally, remember that early in the season or after a long layoff from the game, it's often difficult to sustain the mental endurance you'll need for 18 holes. However, if you understand and plan for ways to cope with mental and physical fatigue, you'll be able to cope with those first rounds much better. Remember, technique isn't always the culprit when things go wrong!

Chapter 7

THE SWING'S THE THING

From time to time, it's always a good idea to take a look at your swing. That might mean shooting some video or asking your local professional to help out. In either case, it's important to understand how the swing works—and what to look for in yours!

Good trajectory, curvature, face contact, and impact are all the results of—you guessed it—a good golf swing! The anchors of a good swing are:

- The swing plane

- Body pivot

- The release

These three areas control your swing and whether the shot goes straight down the fairway or veers off into a water hazard. When these "anchors" are in synch, the swing is a finely tuned machine. However, if something gets out of whack, it can be hard to keep the ball on the fairway.

THE SWING PLANE

The angle of the club as it swings back and through is one of the most important factors in producing correct contact, curvature, and trajectory. It's also *the* key to making the ball go farther, something every golfer desires! This angle is commonly known as the swing plane. To play good, consistent golf, the swing plane must remain constant from shot-to-shot and club-to-club.

Figure 26
Matching the Swing Plane

The initial swing plane is determined at address by the angle of the club as it sits on the ground. Once the club is in motion, it should swing along the plane that was established at address to a point halfway back (hip level). At this point the club should be parallel to the ground and the target line.

As the club continues up to the top of the backswing, it should take an angle that is above and parallel to the original swing plane. As it reaches the top of the swing, the club will again be parallel to the ground and the target line.

The angle of the downswing should simply repeat the path of the backswing—in the opposite direction! As the club starts down, it is above and parallel to the original swing plane. Half way down (hip level), it is again parallel to the ground and the target line. The club should continue to retrace its path as it approaches impact, moving back up the original swing plane on the other side of the ball to the finish.

Because the swing plane is established at address, it's important that you have:

- **Clubs that fit:** If your clubs are too short or too long, too upright or flat, your posture at address will be affected. As a result, your swing will be "out of plane" right from the start.

- **A proper set up**: Good body position at address is the foundation for a swing that is "on plane." In your set-up:

  o Keep your weight positioned toward the balls of your feet

  o Bend from the hips so that your shoulders are in line with your toes

  o Your knees should be slightly flexed

  o Your arms should hang comfortably away from your body

Clubs that fit and a good body position at address allows the club to set at the proper angle at address. Remember that the varying length and lie of every club will produce a different swing plane angle. Shorter clubs will have a more upright swing plane while longer clubs (like the driver) will have a flatter swing plane angle.

Figure 27
Drive Setup and Wedge Setup

BODY PIVOT

The motion of the body back and through the swing is the second swing "anchor." As with the swing plane, the position of the body at address is a critical factor in making a good pivot away from and through the ball.

Figure 28
Proper Body Pivot

During the backswing, the upper body starts the motion as the lower body resists or remains "quiet." The shoulders turn back on the angle the body established at address. The left shoulder moves down and underneath the chin as the right shoulder moves up and back. As the shoulders continue to turn, weight is shifted by the lower body from the center to the right foot, knee, and gluteus maximus. Bends or flexes at the hips and knees should remain constant throughout the backswing.

During the downswing, the body simply moves in the opposite direction. The downswing starts from the ground up. The feet, knees, and hips begin to shift weight from the right side back to the left side. Initially, the movement is lateral, however, it becomes a turning motion as the left hip starts to clear. The right knee moves down and toward the back of the left knee, and the right heel slowly begins to move up and off the ground.

As your weight shifts, your upper body remains turned and "quiet." As

Figure 29
Proper Impact and Release

your lower body continues to clear and your arms and hands swing the club through impact, your shoulders turn through on the same axis on which they turned back. At impact, your weight has shifted predominantly back to the left side and your hips have cleared and are open to the target line.

At the finish, almost all of your body's weight has shifted to the outside of your left foot. Your hips have turned through so that your belt buckle faces the target and your right thigh is touching your left thigh. Your right heel has lifted off of the ground, allowing your right foot to finish straight up and down.

Figure 30
Balance Finish

THE RELEASE

The release is the third and possibly the most important swing "anchor." In the end, impact is the only thing that really matters. However, consistently good impact is generally the result of a consistently "good" golf swing.

During the release, uncock your wrists as your left arm and hand rotate to the target. With a neutral grip, the back of your left hand should face the target at impact, resulting in a "square" clubface at impact. You should concentrate on rotating your left forearm and the last three fingers of your left hand toward the target to keep the clubface "square" at impact.

The left hand creates the hitting motion, the right hand supports that motion. The right hand simply mirrors the motion of the left hand. More specifically, the pressures from the right palm on the left thumb and that of the "V" formed by the right thumb and the index finger should remain constant. These two "pressure points" help to absorb impact as it is created by the left forearm and hand.

A sound release creates a square clubface. A square clubface results in a straight shot. But what happens if the clubface isn't square at impact? If it's open, the result will be a slice. If it's shut, the result will be a hook. If you are slicing or hooking, jump back to Chapter 5 and take a look at the chart. Then get back to work using the drills in Chapter 6.

Speaking of drills, maybe it's time to think about more than just *what* you need to work on, but also *how* you do that work. You'll find some suggestions for the *how* in Chapter 9.

Chapter 8

THE DRIVER

Most golfers love to hit with the driver. It's the club they spend the most time with on the practice tee and, after a round, it's the shots they hit with their driver that golfers love to talk about.

Nearly everyone wants to drive the ball longer and straighter. To do that, The Four Keys can play a big part. But there are some other factors that can make the difference between a sliced drive that lands out of bounds and a booming drive down the middle of the fairway. So let's take a look at hitting the driver straighter, then longer.

HITTING STRAIGHTER DRIVES

A straight drive is the result of a swing that is on plane, has the proper body pivot, takes the correct path to the ball during the downswing and has

Figure 31
Driver From Behind

Figure 32
Driver From Front

a club face in the process of release as contact is made with the ball. Whew! That's asking a lot. But all of those things are necessary for a shot to go down the middle of the fairway.

Optimally, at impact the driver strikes the back inside quadrant of the ball. And unlike hitting the ball with an iron, the driver requires a motion that sweeps the ball off of the tee, rather than colliding with the ground. In fact, a downward hit with the driver can not only result in a bad shot, but can also damage the top of the driver!

Ball Position

Something as simple as the position of the ball at address can be the difference between driving the ball well or spending the day searching for your ball. Because of the sweeping motion used with the driver, the ball should be positioned even with the left eye (for a right-handed golfer). This is more forward in the stance than the position of the ball used for iron shots and is more toward the center of the stance.

Swing Plane

Swinging the club "on plane" is necessary to make the correct ball contact at impact. In general terms, the club should swing up and over your right shoulder during the backswing and over the left shoulder at the finish. With the ball elevated off of the ground at address, a slightly flat or lower than the right shoulder swing is better a better mistake than one that's too upright or straight up and down.

If you have an upright swing, try a practice swing with the club head positioned at knee level. Let the club swing back and through at the same height that it used at address. This helps create the proper arc necessary to make a more level, sweeping motion at impact.

You can also make better impact with your driver by how you tee the ball. The "rule of thumb" for teeing the ball states that half the ball should be visible above the club head at address. If your swing is flatter, tee the ball slightly higher. If your swing is upright, tee the ball down.

Pivot

Body pivot plays a crucial role in creating the correct, level motion into impact. At address, right-handed golfers should shift slightly more weight to their right foot. As the club swings back, the upper body should turn as more weight shifts to the right leg. At the top of the backswing, more than 80 percent of the body's weight should be positioned onto the right foot, knee and glute. The head should shift slightly to the right of the ball, as well.

On the downswing, it's critical that the back stay facing the target as the downswing begins. This feeling helps the player make contact with the back inside quadrant of the ball. Weight should begin to shift back to the left side starting with a lateral movement of the feet and knees with the hips following through to impact and the finish.

Again, the most important thing to remember is to keep your back turned and facing the target as you start the downswing. This helps slot the club to the inside. Hitting from outside the target line on the downswing is a recipe for disaster!

The Release

The release is the final component in producing a straighter drive. Using a proper grip, the back of the left hand should face the target at impact. This releases the club face so that the club can square up as it approaches contact.

Swings that are too upright tend to come from having the side of the left hand facing the target at impact. This results in a slice. To help correct this problem make a practice swing at knee level. Feel the start of the downswing coming from inside the target line. Try to feel how the left hand and forearm rotate prior to impact.

Flat swings usually result in hooks. By letting the club swing more over the right shoulder during the backswing while attempting to turn through the shot with better form (with the waist and lower body), most hooks should disappear.

Hitting Longer Drives

Hitting "big" drives is a result of hitting the ball more consistently in the sweet spot, having the correct angle at impact, and, of course, club head speed. Hitting the ball in the sweet spot can help even players with less club head speed hit the ball further just by hitting the center of the club face more often!

The angle of approach at impact is also important. The most direct blow to the ball is produced by coming slightly from the inside of the target line at impact. If the club is cutting across the ball (too much inside or outside the target line), it will produce a glancing blow and reduced club head speed.

Club Head Speed

Club head speed is necessary for distance. Keep in mind that there is a big difference between speed and strength. Strength helps, but speed is necessary. Some golfers are born with speed. They have an abundance of fast twitch muscles. This is how a petite person can hit the ball farther than a bigger, stronger person. I like to use the analogy of a tight end and a wide receiver in football. A wide receiver can be turned into a tight end by making him bigger and stronger. But rarely can a tight end be turned into a receiver. They usually don't possess enough speed. Speed can, however, be created in a couple of ways.

The first way is to make sure that the player is making a full swing. The club must reach a level at least parallel to the top of the backswing. If it is slightly longer, that's even better—provided the club, arms, and body are all in synch. There should be a full finish as well to allow the club to finish across the back of the head with the lower body turned through and facing the target.

The second method is to create more "swish" in the swing. Hold the club up off the ground and swing back and through. The club should create a "swishing" sound as it whizzes through the air. The louder the sound, the more speed has been created.

I encourage my students to create a loud as sound as possible while remaining in balance. It's the ultimate test of each individual's swing speed and is a great way to test their club face speed potential.

This is also an excellent drill for improving swing speed. There are lots of great devices on the market today that measure club head speed. Get access to one, measure your club head speed, and then spend some time each practice session on improving your club head speed. A ball or course isn't even necessary! Simply spend ten to fifteen minutes making practice swings up off the ground, creating louder and louder "swishing" sounds while staying in balance. Measure yourself monthly and you'll be surprised. An improvement of only 1 MPH is equal to 2.5 to 3 yards of distance. So give yourself permission to speed up!

Finding the "Right" Driver

Clubs DO make a difference. 460cc driver heads have been proven to be the longest, most efficient club heads on the market. Developments that have made it possible to adjust loft, lie, and face angle make a big difference as well. But for all the technology, it's still important to choose the driver that looks and feels good to you.

Most club heads come in lofts from 8.5 to 10.5 degrees. Choose a loft that best suits your ball flight. The ball should climb and then level out as it reaches its peak flight. "Sky balls" and line drives aren't good results. Additionally, if your ball looks like it is falling out of the sky you have a club head with too little loft to support your swing speed. Conversely, if the ball is shooting straight up into the air, the driver has too much loft.

For most golfers 8.5 to 10.5 degrees of loft is adequate. However, many companies now also produce drivers with lofts up to 13 degrees to help ladies, juniors, seniors, or other golfers with slower club head speeds get the ball into the air. The important thing is to find the driver that produces the optimal ball flight for your swing.

One more thing. Get fitted for your clubs by a professional. Don't guess or leave anything to chance. Invest in a fitting by a club manufacturer's rep, certified club fitter or PGA Professional. He or she will help you find the driver that is right for you!

Chapter 9

PRACTICE REALLY DOES MAKE PERFECT

"Nobody's a natural. You work hard to get good and then work to get better." – Paul Coffey, NHL Hall of Fame

When golf legend Byron Nelson was a professional at Reading Country Club in Reading, Pennsylvania, he often saw the same lady member on the range. She always practiced the same way, hitting only her seven-iron. As a result, she was a very good ball striker.

One day Byron walked down to the range and asked her, "Why are you spending all of your time practicing the same way? Don't you know that to become a better golfer you must practice the things that aren't your strengths?"

It doesn't matter if you are young or old. There is only one way to improve your game—practice. And although repetition is a great way to improve, how and what you practice are equally, if not more important.

There are many ways to practice the game of golf. You can practice to:

- Improve your technique

- Develop rhythm

- Ingrain a good feeling

- Improve a specific part of your game

Practicing to improve your technique requires the most dedication. It takes lots of repetitions to work through ingrained mistakes. However, the good news is that those repetitions can take many forms:

- Hitting balls

- Making practice swings in the mirror

- Videoing your swing

- Taking a few moments to sit and visualize the swing in your mind

- Making swings without a ball

The most effective way to improve technique is to use a combination of all of the methods outlined above. And because everyone learns and processes information differently, there is no "magic" number of repetitions that will guarantee success. It's important instead, to keep making repetitions until you become familiar with the technique you are attempting to ingrain.

Good rhythm is all "feel." Every golfer has an internal clock that establishes the rhythm of their swing. Many players are right on target when they talk about "getting too quick" during their swing. Hitting good shots means that the player has matched up their body, club, arms and hands at impact. If one part moves too fast or is out of synch, the swing will feel "quick." Often golfers destroy their rhythm just when they're beginning to really establish it. Many a golfer hitting solid seven-irons that travel 150 yards with a smooth, uniform swing, has ruined their rhythm (and their swing) by attempting to gain an extra ten yards by swinging harder and faster. Once you have established the pace and swing length that works for you, don't deviate from it. Try to replicate that exact feeling over and over again.

Every player has strengths and weaknesses. Don't spend all of your practice time on your strengths (like Byron Nelson's lady member!). Be honest with yourself and work on your weaknesses until they become your strengths. When your game is well rounded, an off day (for example trouble getting off the tee), won't impact your score as much because you can use other parts of your game (like putting) to compensate.

Now that we've discussed what to practice, it's time to hone in on the "how." Remember, practice isn't just about time. How and how often are just as important.

LENGTH OF PRACTICE

Practice length is never as important as practice quality. Quality is achieved by setting goals for every session and then measuring yourself against those goals.

I like to divide practice time into three equal parts. For example, if you have two hours to practice, I would divide that time into three sessions, covering three specific areas (i.e., putting, chipping, full swing). Each session should last 35 minutes with breaks between the sessions. Allowing yourself to take breaks will help you to remain fresh so you can use the session to do more than just "beat balls."

FREQUENCY OF PRACTICE

Obviously, it would be great to practice every day, but too much practice can also lead to "burn out." Taking a day off once in a while is a good idea. Getting practice in also doesn't mean that you have to head out to the course or the range. You can putt indoors, swing in front of a mirror, or just make swings without a ball.

Visualizing your swing is also a great way to practice when you can't get out. Sitting quietly, simply visualize the swing you want to make — or maybe the smooth stroke you love — with your putter. Another way to use visualization is in preparing for competition. Just play the course in your head—shot by shot, putt by putt—and "see" that great round take shape. Finally, it's also productive to remember good shots you've hit, like a great bunker shot or putt. These "reminders" will help you to feel relaxed and confident when faced with similar situations in the future.

WHAT TO PRACTICE

One of the best ways to determine what you should practice is to review your most recent rounds. What did you do well? What parts of your game added to your score? Once you've targeted your weaknesses choose three areas from the following list to work on during your practice session:

- Full swing

- Distance wedges

- Pitching

- Chipping

- Sand play

- Lag putting

- Short putts

At the end of the each session, grade your performance on a scale of 1-5 as follows:

- Disaster

- Needs improvement

- Average

- Very good

- Best ever

Once you've cycled through all seven categories, pick the three categories with your lowest score and focus on them during your next session. Cycle through them again, repeating the process.

This is the strategy I used to help 1998 U.S. Amateur Champion Hank Kuehne prepare for the 1999 U.S. Open. It allowed him work in every area of his game and kept him mentally fresh. The regimen must have worked as Hank was the only amateur to make the cut and was the low amateur for the event.

WHEN YOU DON'T HAVE TIME

Just because you don't have a lot of time doesn't mean you can't get better! And although you should keep your weaknesses at the top of the list, the best places to concentrate when time is short are on ball striking and putting. You can hit balls on the range, work in the mirror to refine technique, or make practice swings to improve how you hit the ball.

Work on the speed of your putts when you don't have time for a full practice session. Speed is usually the first thing that suffers when players don't have time to practice. All you'll need is someplace to hit a putt—you don't need a hole. Putt to the edge of the green (or even a wall) focusing on pace, length of the stroke and making solid contact.

If you don't have much time before you play a round of golf, make sure that your first stop is the putting green. Practice hitting putts of 20 to 30 feet to a hole or the edge of the green. All that you want to establish is the speed of the greens and the rhythm of your stroke. Then head to the first tee.

When you get there, spend a few minutes making practice swings, first with a wedge, then a seven-iron and finally the driver. All you want to do is wake up your golf muscles and establish the rhythm of your swing. You'll get in more swings than if you were headed to the range. And you'll start the round more confidently without the memory of hurried, missed shots on the range.

PRACTICE CAN BE FUN!

Practice doesn't have to be drudgery! Following are some games you can play that will help you to have fun while you're improving your game.

- *Play the Course on the Range:* Simulate the shots you'd need to play your favorite golf course. You can simulate the direction you would need to aim, avoid "hazards" and even punch out of the "trees."

- *Around the Horn:* This is a great putting drill. Pick a hole on the practice green that's on a subtle slope. Place four balls, starting at three feet from the hole, around the hole at the twelve, three, six, and nine o'clock positions. After you make all four putts without missing, increase the distance to four feet. If you miss a putt, begin all over again at three feet.

- *Up and Down:* Take five balls and position them around the edge of the green. The goal is to hit all five balls close enough to the hole that you can get "up and down" with one putt. Give yourself two points for every hole that you get "up and down" with one putt. If you chip the ball in, you can two-putt one hole. Try and score a total of ten points before you leave the green. (This could take a while!)

- *Fairway Drill:* Simulate a fairway that is 30-40 yards wide on the driving range. Practice hitting fourteen balls onto the "fairway." Keep track of the number of fairways you hit.

- *Lag Putting Drill:* Place four tees in a circle three feet from the hole. Start 20 feet from the hole and try to putt all five balls to a spot within the circle. Once you've done that, move to 25 feet and try to hit four out of five balls into the circle. At 35 feet go for three out of five, at 40 feet two out of five.

Chapter 10

FOUR STRATEGIES FOR SUCCESS ON THE COURSE

With a good understanding of the Four Keys, you're ready to begin shooting lower scores letting you enjoy the game a lot more. But playing the game entails more than just great ball striking. To play well all of the time, you'll need to incorporate these four simple strategies for success into your game.

USE THE TEE BOX TO YOUR ADVANTAGE

Every tee box provides golfers with the opportunity to have "ball in hand." As in billiards, when the ball is "scratched," golfers can position the ball anywhere within and up to two club lengths behind the tee makers. Again, as in billiards, where you place the ball can make it easier or harder to make a successful shot. The following are some simple strategies that will help you use the tee box to hit more fairways and greens.

1. *Give your shot some room*: Look at how your shot is shaped.
    Did you hit a draw? A fade? Or were your shots straight as
    an arrow? The important thing is to make sure that you give
    your shot the greatest "margin for error" possible.
    For players who like to draw the ball, this means teeing up on
    the left side of the tee box, aiming toward the right side of the
    fairway.
    This leaves almost the entire fairway open for the ball to draw

Figure 33
Proper Positioning Off the Tee with Wind

into.

For players who hit fades, the opposite is true. Tee off from the right side of the box, aiming toward the left side of the fairway. And for "straight shooters," the middle of the box is always the best place.

2. *Tee off from the side of trouble:* Bunkers, water, and other hazards can sometimes appear intimidating when standing on the tee box. One way of taking them out of play is to tee off from the side the trouble is on, aiming away from the hazard. For example, if there is water on the right side of the hole, tee the ball on the right side and aim to the left side of the fairway.

3. *Use the wind*: The best strategy for shots into a cross-wind is to tee off on the side opposite as direction of the wind,

aiming back into it. The idea is to use the wind as a backstop, allowing it to push the ball back toward the center of the fairway. Therefore, if the wind is from the right, tee off from the left side of the box and aim to the right. From the left, tee off from the right side of the box and aim to the left.

MINIMIZE YOUR MISTAKES

Even the best players get into trouble sometimes. The important thing is to not let that mistake escalate from a potential bogey to a triple bogey, or worse. So, "take your medicine" and get the ball back into play! To do that, simply:

1. *Play the percentages:* Analyze the situation and play the highest percentage recovery shot available. That might mean

Figure 34
Punching Out of Trees

chipping out of the trees to get back onto the fairway instead of attempting to hit a shot through a six-inch gap, or playing sideways out of a bunker with a steep lip.

2. *Avoid the obstacles:* Find the route out of trouble that avoids leaves, branches, trees, stones, rocks, or anything else that might get in the way. A clear route will provide the highest success rate and fewer "big" numbers on your scorecard.

Pick the Pins

Players who hit lots of greens in regulation shoot low scores. Tour players hit an average of 11.5 greens in regulation; weekend warriors who shoot in the 90s average just two. Although skill and great ball striking is definitely a major reason for the difference, it's just as important to know when to aim at the pin, and when to choose the center of the green.

I like to color code pin placements using the colors in a traffic light.

Figure 35
Identifying the 'Go Zone'

Green for "go," yellow for "caution," and red for "stop." A pin placed in the center of the green is definitely a "green" placement. Take dead aim and "go" for it.

Yellow pins favor one side of the green and might be close to a bunker or a water hazard. Be "cautious," and aim toward the fat part of the green.

Pin positions where even the slightest miss will send the ball into a hazard are "red." "Stop," aim at the center of the green, and two-putt from thirty to forty feet.

Using this strategy, you'll hit more greens, put less strain on your short game, and lower your scores.

SOLIDIFY YOUR SHORT GAME

A great short game can make up for missing greens, but three-putts and two-chips can ruin a day of great ball striking. The following are some simple ways to improve your short game and minimize those extra shots around the green.

- *Three putts:* Good putts are a combination of the right direction and the right distance. To ensure the ball goes on the right line, your body and, even more importantly, your eyes, should be parallel to the target line. If your eyes are pointed to the left or right of the target, the putter will swing to the left or right as well.

  A good example of this occurred during the first round of the 1998 Masters. Mark O'Meara was struggling with his putting. His coach (and my boss at the time), Hank Haney, noticed that Mark's eyes were pointed to the right of his intended target at address. Hank held Mark's head, keeping his eyes parallel to the target line, for a few strokes on the practice green. Mark's putting improved instantly and he went on to win the event. Distance control is a bit more difficult. It's important to control both the length and pace of the stroke. I recommend that players read the putt, address the ball, and then focus solely on hitting the putt at the proper speed.

A good drill for this is to putt to the edge of the green. Start 20 feet away and putt to the edge. Your only target is the edge of the green. As you get a feel for the distance, alternate between shorter and longer putts, adding uphill and downhill lies as well. The goal is to focus solely on the length and pace of the stroke required to hit the ball just to the edge of the green.

- *Two chips:* Players who have to hit the ball twice to reach the green from inside 40 yards won't shoot low scores. These two-chips are usually caused by bad shot selection, weak technique, or a lack of "touch."

  To improve shot selection, I recommend players concentrate on getting the ball onto the green every time. It doesn't matter if the ball is close to the hole, it's more important to just get the ball onto the putting surface.

  Players should pay close attention to the lie to determine the shot they should play. If there's a cushion, a pitch shot might be the answer, if the lie is "tight," chip the ball instead.

  Chip shots can be played with clubs ranging from a seven-iron down to a sand wedge. Your choice should be based on how far the ball needs to travel. To hit a good chip:

  o Take a narrow stance

  o Play the ball back in your stance, inside your right foot

  o Stand closer to the ball ensuring that the shaft of the club is straight up and down. It's okay for the heel of the club to be off of the ground for this shot.

Figure 36
Chip Shot

o Keep your hands and weight forward and toward the left
leg (for a right-hander).

This setup creates a descending blow which induces the ball
to roll. The motion should be similar to a putt, with the hands
remaining in front of the ball at impact. The swing should be
short, with the hands not moving past the right thigh on the
backswing or the left thigh as the club moves through the ball.

Pitch shots are usually played with the sand wedge. To hit this
shot, make sure your lie has a cushion of grass, as the bottom or
bounce of the club will strike the ground at impact. To set up for

this shot:

- o Take a stance that is a little wider than used for the chip. Your heels should be inside your armpits.

- o The ball should be in the center of your stance with your hands even with the ball.

Figure 37
Pitch Shot

- o Your weight should be evenly balanced.

Pitches are simply a smaller version of the full swing. During the takeaway, however, the club should swing up the shaft plane established at address with the toe of the club pointing to the sky. This face angle provides the necessary clubface loft to pitch the ball into the air.

As the club approaches impact, clubface loft must be maintained so that the bottom or bounce of the club slides underneath the ball. As a general rule, the length of the swing should be the same on both sides of the ball. It's okay for the follow through to be longer than the backswing, but a follow through that's shorter than the backswing is usually a recipe for trouble.

Once you've mastered your chipping and pitching technique, it's time to work on touch. Practice making swings to hit the ball specific distances. For example, make a swing with your sand wedge that reaches your waist on each side of the ball. Groove this swing and then work to create the same rhythm for shots of different lengths.

Using these four simple strategies, you'll keep the ball in play, hit more greens, minimize shots around the green, and get out of trouble quickly and consistently.   And they'll help you break 100, 90, 80, 70—whatever your goal may be.

Chapter 11

A STUDENT'S STORY

Throughout this book I've provided examples of world class players I have observed or taught—and how the skills I've described helped them to improve their games and *win*. But the knowledge in this book isn't just for "the best." This advice works equally well for week-end, municipal golfers, country club players junior golfers, and even beginners. In fact, any golfer can benefit from the techniques that I recommend in this book.

Since I started this book with a story, it's only fitting that the book should end with a story. A story that any player at any level can relate to.

Fifteen years ago I was Director of Instruction at the Hank Haney Golf Ranch in McKinney, Texas. Every afternoon a lady in her early forties would come and hit balls at the far left side of the driving range. She was always in the same spot at the same time—every day.

She practiced hard but she didn't have very good technique and she didn't have much club head speed. Occasionally, while I was teaching, I'd glance over to watch her swing. She was swinging hard, but not getting any results. The bottom line was that, for all of her practice, she wasn't getting any better. It therefore took me by surprise one evening when the shop attendant told me I had a lesson tomorrow with "the lady at the end of the range."

The next day I met Deb Mielke, "the lady at the end of the range." We talked for a while about her goals. She told me that she shot some pretty good scores, but from my distant assessment, it appeared that she would struggle to break 95. She wanted to see just how good she could be and had an ultimate goal of qualifying for the USGA Senior Women's Amateur

Championship when she turned 50.

What I remember from that first lesson is that her six-irons carried only 100 yards in the air. I asked her if she could swing the club any faster so that the ball would travel higher in the air and carry a bit further. She tried, but, the ball didn't go any higher or further.

I explained to her that we had some work to do to make her ultimate goal realistic. Deb was committed to improving and told me she was willing to work on her game. Little did I know that she had been scouting our instructors for a few months and had settled on me for the job of helping her to accomplish her goal.

After that first lesson, Deb had a standing appointment at 11 every Friday morning. Initially, most of our work was on her full swing – and I used the Four Keys as the basis for her improvement plan. Over time we touched on every aspect of her game and made significant changes in how she approached the game.

Over the last fifteen years Deb improved—a lot! She won her club championship twice, accomplished her goal of qualifying for the USGA Senior Women's Amateur Championship, and along the way qualified for six USGA Women's Mid-Amateur Championships as well as a USGA Women's Four Ball Championship. She was the Senior Medalist at the Women's Trans National and has been a top ten finisher at the North South Senior Women's Championship, the Texas Women's Open Senior Division, and the Texas Senior Amateur Championship. Additionally, Deb recently won the San Antonio Regional Championship – Women's Senior Division.

Deb's success has certainly been based on hard work. More important, Deb has learned to analyze her shot trajectory, curvature, club face contact, and impact. This allows her to self-diagnose and fix swing flaws when she's on the range or even in the middle of a competitive round. Using the Four Keys, she's been able to turn around practice sessions—and tournament rounds—that weren't going the way she wanted them to.

Deb and I don't see each other every Friday anymore. She's on a new level. When we do get together I find, without fail, that her swing has improved. She frequently says that understanding the Four Keys made a world of difference for her. She never gets lost anymore. Even if she's a little off, all she has to do is take a step back and analyze her shots. Then using the chart (from Chapter 5), she determines the probable cause and gets back on track.

No matter how well or much you play, you too can improve. Improvement starts with a plan—a plan that you can build based on analysis of your shots using the Four Keys. Using that plan, you too can work to minimize and eventually eliminate mishits that are adding strokes to your game.

The Four Keys to Improving Your Game, is the road out of confusion. It's also the road to better golf. Be patient and stick to the plan you've established. Golf is the greatest game of all and I hope that after reading this book you'll enjoy improving and playing YOUR game.

1   *Glenn Mahler, Head Fitter, Titleist Fitting Works Tour Van*

ABOUT THE AUTHOR

Tim Cusick serves as the Director of Golf Instruction at the award-winning Four Seasons Resort and Club and the acclaimed Four Seasons Golf School. Cusick joined the Four Seasons in 2005.

He formerly managed the golf instruction staff for Hank Haney Golf, Inc. where he was in charge of hiring and training the golf staff at seven different facilities in Texas including the complex known as the Hank Haney Golf Ranch in McKinney, Texas. He worked closely with the renowned golf teacher for twenty-three years. He also has previous experience at well-known golf facilities including: PGA West Resort Courses, Alta Mesa Country Club, Elk River Golf Club, and Pinehurst Hotel and Country Club. Cusick also served as Assistant Men's Golf Coach at Southern Methodist University from 1993 to 1997.

Under Tim's stewardship, more than one hundred junior golfers have secured college golf scholarships. He has coached players that have won on all the major professional golf tours around the world. Tim has coached: Bruce Crampton, Michael Allen, Brad Elder, Ilhee-Lee, Kelli Kuehne, Hank Kuehne, Kris Tschetter, Hollis Stacy, and Sandra Palmer as well as world class amateurs Trip Kuehne and Dallas Cowboys quarterback, Tony Romo. He has coached the PGA National Junior Champion and members of the U.S. and European Curtis Cup teams.

Cusick travels worldwide to train other golf instructors to improve their craft through his Coaching Champions™ seminars. His seminars have been conducted in Denmark, Korea, Germany, Sweden, and Mexico as well as at the Four Seasons Resort and Club.

He is an accredited member of the PGA of America since 1989. He wa
named a Best Teacher in Texas by Golf Digest (2001, 2011-2012, 201:
2014), Top Teacher in the South Central Region by Golf Magazine (2005
06), Best Public Facility Teacher by AvidGolfer (2002). In 2005 and 2009
he was awarded Teacher of the Year by the Northern Texas PGA as well
as Teacher of the Year for the Metro Chapter of the Northern Texas PGA
In 2014 he was awarded the NTPGA Horton Smith Award for education.

He has been a regular contributor to AvidGolfer magazine in Dallas-
Fort Worth. He has also contributed columns to Golf for Women, Golf Tips
Magazine, Golf Illustrated, The PGA Magazine, and Celeb Life. Additionally,
he has been a featured guest on The Golf Channel, ESPN, The Golfer's Home,
Sirius XM Radio, and Fox Sports Radio.